Favorite Songs of Praise

Solos, Duets, Trios with Optional Piano Accompaniment

Arranged by Michael Lawrence

MW00575046

CONTENTS

Alfred

© 2009 Alfred Music Publishing Co., Inc.
All Rights Reserved. Printed in USA.

ISBN-10: 0-7390-6655-2
ISBN-13: 978-0-7390-6655-3

Cover photo courtesy of Bill Davenport

ABOVE ALL

CLARINET

Words and Music by
PAUL BALOCHE and LENNY LEBLANC
Arranged by MICHAEL LAWRENCE

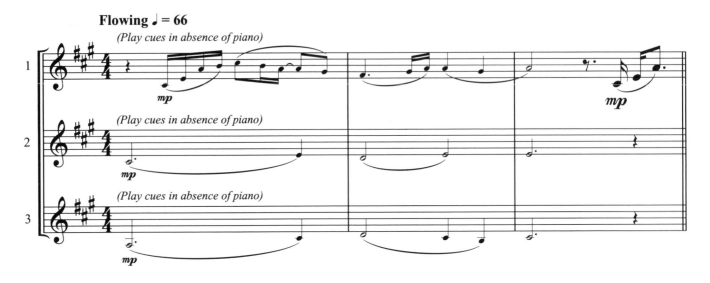

4

BLESSED BE YOUR NAME

Words and Music by
BETH REDMAN and MATT REDMAN
Arranged by MICHAEL LAWRENCE

32732

6

COME, NOW IS THE TIME TO WORSHIP

Words and Music by
BRIAN DOERKSEN
Arranged by MICHAEL LAWRENCE

With energy ♩ = 112-116

DRAW ME CLOSE

Words and Music by
KELLY CARPENTER
Arranged by MICHAEL LAWRENCE

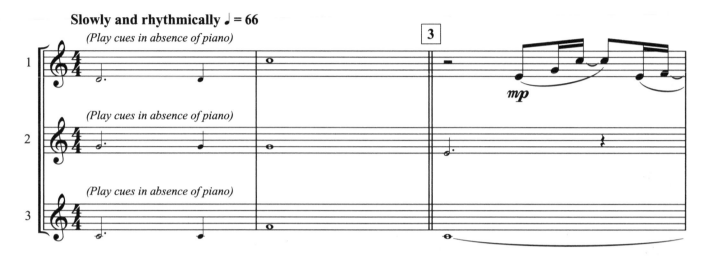

HERE I AM TO WORSHIP
(LIGHT OF THE WORLD)

Words and Music by
TIM HUGHES
Arranged by MICHAEL LAWRENCE

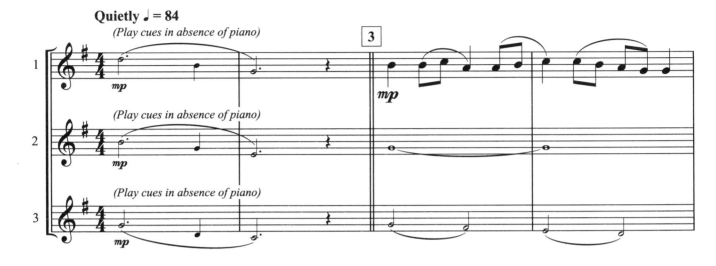

To Coda ⊕

21

mf

mf

mf

HOW DEEP THE FATHER'S LOVE FOR US

Words and Music by
STUART TOWNEND
Arranged by MICHAEL LAWRENCE

Slowly and simply ♩ = 66

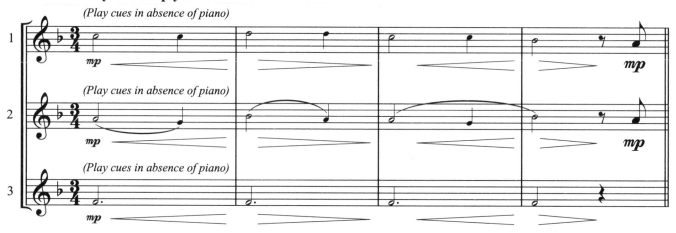

HOW GREAT IS OUR GOD

Words and Music by
JESSE REEVES, CHRIS TOMLIN and ED CASH
Arranged by MICHAEL LAWRENCE

I COULD SING OF YOUR LOVE FOREVER

Words and Music by
MARTIN SMITH
Arranged by MICHAEL LAWRENCE

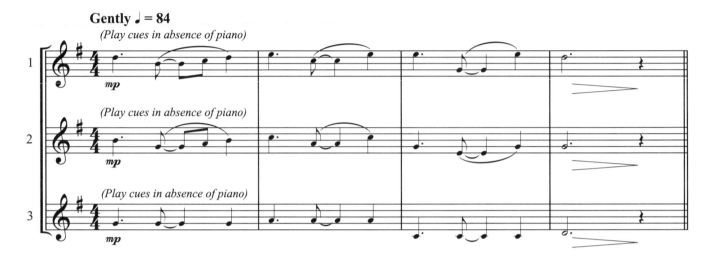

IN CHRIST ALONE
(MY HOPE IS FOUND)

Words and Music by
STUART TOWNEND and KEITH GETTY
Arranged by MICHAEL LAWRENCE

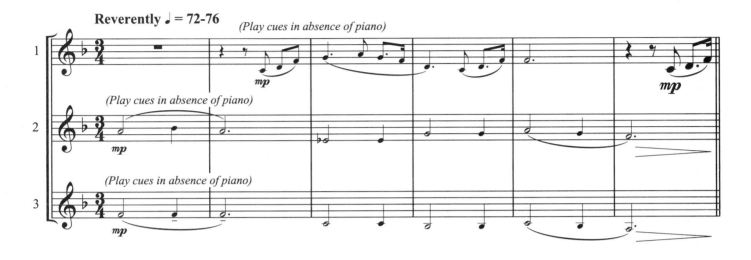

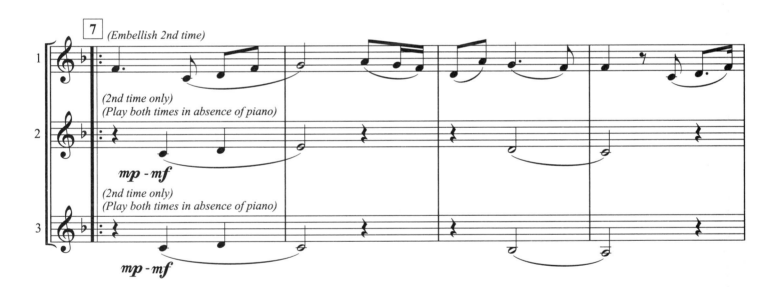

28

32732

LORD I LIFT YOUR NAME ON HIGH

Words and Music by
RICK FOUNDS
Arranged by MICHAEL LAWRENCE

(Play cues in absence of piano)

MY SAVIOR, MY GOD

Words and Music by
AARON SHUST
Arranged by MICHAEL LAWRENCE

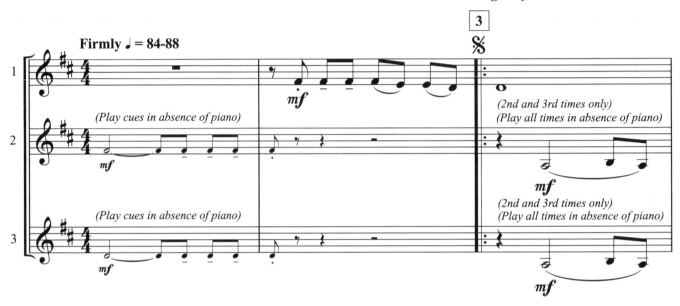

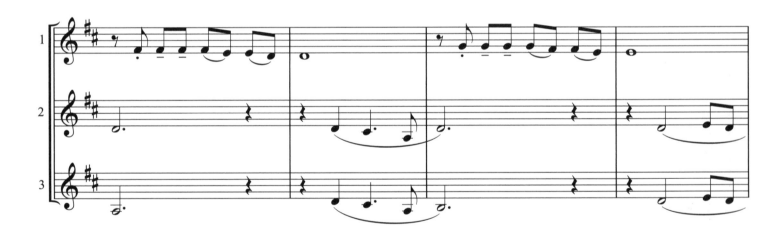

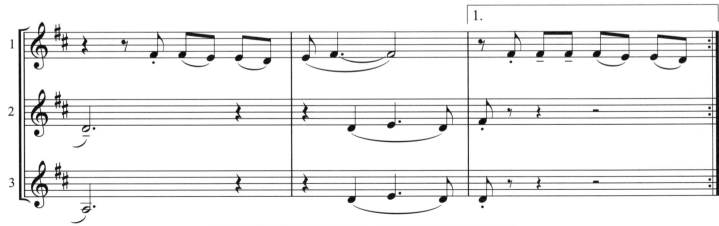

2nd time To Coda ⊕

D.S. 𝄋 al Coda

⊕ Coda

THERE IS A REDEEMER

Words and Music by
MELODY GREEN
Arranged by MICHAEL LAWRENCE

Gently ♩ = 80

(Play cues in absence of piano)

(Play cues in absence of piano)

(Play cues in absence of piano)

mp

(2nd time only)
(Play both times in absence of piano)
mp

(2nd time only)
(Play both times in absence of piano)
mp

mf

mf

mf

32732

THERE IS A REDEEMER

Words and Music by
MELODY GREEN
Arranged by MICHAEL LAWRENCE